Motivation ESL Workbook
A Gentle Guide to Confidence, Growth, and Encouragement for English Learners

Dara K. Fulton

Purpose of this workbook

The purpose of this workbook is for students to build their confidence as they grow as adult learners in learning English as a Second Language (ESL). The exercises, activities, and readings in this workbook will help inspire students in their learning journey. Activities will reflect on students' own learning experiences (good or bad), practice their reading and writing skills, all while learning how to navigate and feel comfortable in the learning process.

Who is Dara K. Fulton?

Dara is the founder and ESL teacher of Applied ESL. Applied ESL is an online English tutoring service with a creative approach that helps adult learners build confidence while improving their English-speaking skills. Her tutoring company focuses on the basic and intermediate levels of the English language through conversation, listening, and pronunciation practice with the use of visuals and real-life scenarios. The goal is to help students feel confident to speak English in everyday life. Dara has years' experience teaching English as a Second Language (ESL) to adults. She is passionate about teaching and helping people.

Dara likes to tell her students, "Try your best."

INTRODUCTION

Write your name: _______________________________________

Where are you from? _______________________________________

Is this your first time learning English? (Write YES or NO) ___________

Why do you want to learn English?

Name 1 thing you want to do after learning English?

____

GOAL SETTING: What does this mean?

Goal setting: to set goals for yourself. **Goals** are the things you want to accomplish.

Examples of goals: I want to make money. I want to speak English well. I want to travel to different countries.

Example of goal setting: I will find a full-time job to make more money. I will attend English classes to learn English. I will save money to travel to different countries.

What are your goals? Write your goals

____

____

____

____

____

____

PROMPTS

Prompts are questions, statements, an idea or an image to inspire you to do something. For example: writing

An example of a prompt: **Learning English will help me to…** You will finish the sentence.

You Try: Read the following prompts and finish the sentence

1- Speaking English will help me to…

____

2- Success to me looks like…

____

3- In 2 years, I want to…

____

4 I feel confident in myself when…

____

Look at the pictures below. Which one describes your personality.

Circle the number next to the picture (s)

1

2

3

4

5

MOTIVATION and ENCOURAGEMENT

Read the story about Ms. Alice and her experience learning English, and answer the questions

Ms. Alice (her English name) is an elder Chinese woman who attended an intermediate level English class at a local school. Ms. Alice learned English years ago but didn't have the chance to practice speaking English. Everyone in Ms. Alice's neighborhood speaks Cantonese and Mandarin. When Ms. Alice met her teacher, Ms. Amy, and her classmates, she felt comfortable. She made friends and answered all of Ms. Amy's questions. Ms. Alice did her homework and spoke English well but struggled with grammar. One day, Ms. Amy asked the class to work in pairs. The assignment was to write sentences using the future tense **be going to** and **will**. David and Amy worked together. Amy wrote sentences using *will* but didn't understand how to use ***be going to.***

Amy felt embarrassed and said, "I can't do it!" David said, "It's okay, try your best." Ms. Amy heard what David said and smiled at Amy. She said, "Try your best, because when you try your best, you do your best." Another classmate repeated what Ms. Amy said. Then another student said the same thing. Amy laughed and said, "I am going to try my best tomorrow!" David shouted, "You just said the future!" Ms. Amy said, "See, now you will try your best!"

1- What is the story about?

2- What are the students learning?

3- Why did Ms. Alice feel embarrassed?

4- What does *try your best* mean?

TRUE or FALSE

David laughed at Ms. Alice. _________________

Ms. Amy told Alice to try your best. _________________

Look at the picture. How does it make you feel?

You Try: Read the following prompts and finish the sentence

1- When I try my best, I feel…

____

2- When I feel discouraged, I…

____

3- I feel motivated when…

____

Affirmations: sayings that give us confidence and motivation

Example: **I can learn English. I am improving every day.**

Write 3 affirmations for yourself

1 ____

2 ____

3 ____

Motivation tip: Everyday you won't feel confident. You won't get all the answers right in English. You will feel confused. You will feel tired. Sometimes, you will feel like you're doing well. Every day will be a different day, just like learning English. It's okay to make mistakes, because it is part of learning.

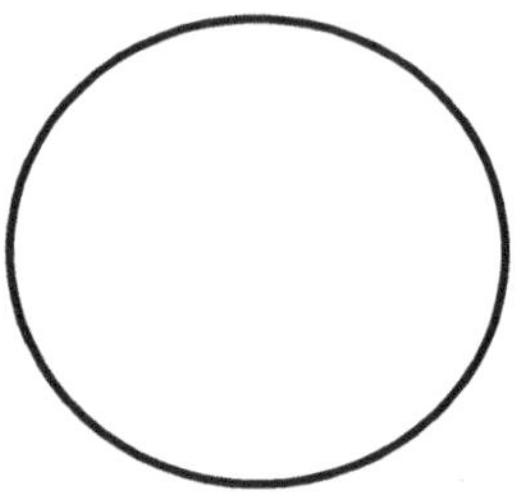 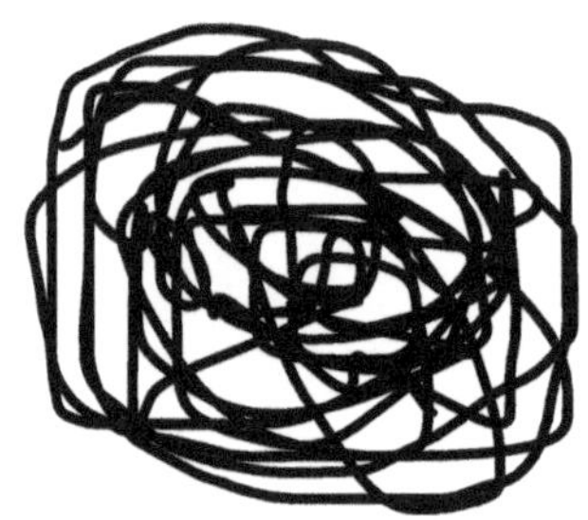 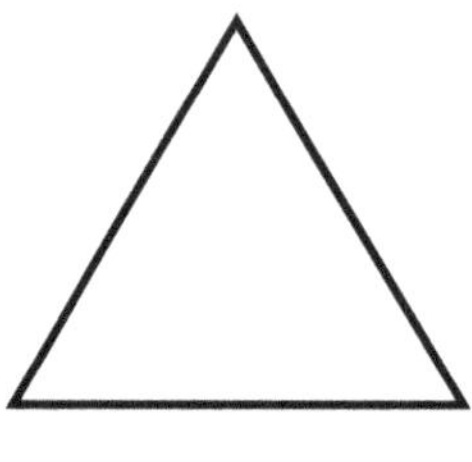

Which one of these do you feel like as an ESL student? The circle, the squiggly circle, or the triangle? Why?

____

____

Finish this sentence: When I don't feel motivated, I…

HOW TO BRAINSTORM

Brainstorm: to think freely to gain ideas about something. We use a **bubble map** to brainstorm.

Bubble Map: a map that helps us get ideas about a topic.

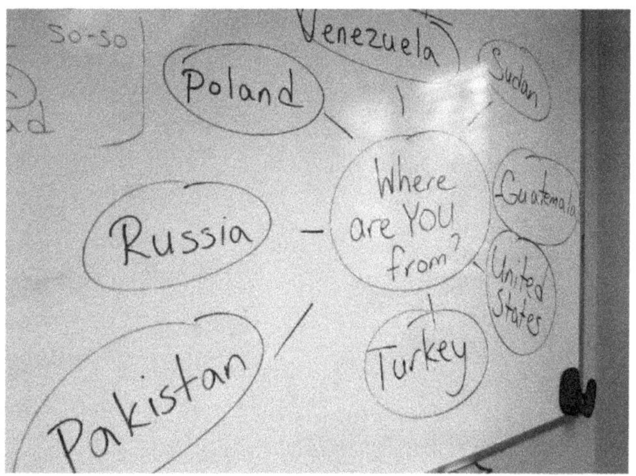

You Try: Complete the bubble map. Write **"In 5 years I will"**

Continue writing your answers from your bubble map here

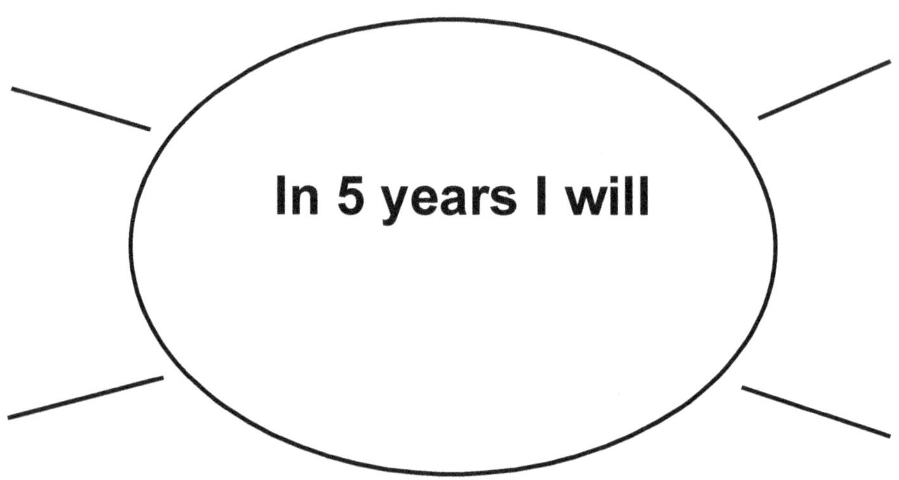

Complete the sentences:

Today, I will…

This week, I will…

This month, I will…

This year, I will**…**

How do YOU try your best?

Read the conversation and answer the questions

A: Learning English is hard! I feel like **quitting**.

B: How long have you been learning English?

A: Six years.

B: Six years? Wow! I have been learning English for 2 years. Why do you want to quit?

A: Because I don't speak like American people.

B: That's okay. It doesn't matter. Just speak clearly and people will understand.

A: Yeah, I know but I don't like grammar. It is confusing! I don't remember the rules.

B: I don't remember the rules either, that is normal. We all make mistakes.

A: I don't know.

B: It's okay to feel discouraged but you should not quit.

A: Well, I will think about it.

Quitting or quit means to give up, to stop

1 Do you think person A will quit learning English? Why?

2 Why does person A want to quit?

3 How many years did person A learn English? ____________________

4 How many years did person B learn English? ____________________

5 Do you have to speak like American people? Why or why not?

Use the next pages to write down and keep track of your English learning progress. You can make copies of these pages for yourself or can share them with your teacher. It's up to you. 😊

<u>YOUR ENGLISH LEARNING CHART</u>

Complete the chart

When did you start learning English?	How many: Months: _______ Years: ________	What is your English level? Beginner ______ Intermediate _____ Advanced ______
Are you currently taking English classes? Yes ____ No _____	Name 1 thing learning English has helped you?	Name 1 or 2 things you can improve on
What do you like learning the most? Speaking _______ Listening ______ Reading _______ Writing ________ Everything 😊 _______	What is difficult for you? Speaking _______ Listening ______ Reading _______ Writing _______	Why are you learning English?

My English Progress Journey

Name: _________________________________ **Date:** _____________________________

MONTH: What I practiced or learned in English

JANUARY	FEBRUARY	MARCH	APRIL
MAY	JUNE	JULY	AUGUST
SEPTEMBER	OCTOBER	NOVEMBER	DECEMBER

My English Month: ___________________________________

This month, I learned:

____

____

Put an x next to your answer

This month, I practiced English by:

Speaking _____

Writing _____

Listening _____

Reading _____

I practiced by:

____

____

New words I learned:

1. _________________________________

2. _________________________________

3. _________________________________

I feel proud because:

____

____

My next goal:

____

____

My English Progress Journey

Name: ______________________________ **Date:** ______________________

MONTH: What I practiced or learned in English

JANUARY	FEBRUARY	MARCH	APRIL
MAY	**JUNE**	**JULY**	**AUGUST**
SEPTEMBER	**OCTOBER**	**NOVEMBER**	**DECEMBER**

My English Month: ______________________________

This month, I learned:

____

____

Put an x next to your answer

This month, I practiced English by:

Speaking _____

Writing _____

Listening ______

Reading ______

I practiced by:

____

____

New words I learned:

1. ______________________________

2. ______________________________

3. ______________________________

I feel proud because:

____

____

My next goal:

____

____

My English Progress Journey

Name: _________________________________   **Date:** _____________________________

MONTH: What I practiced or learned in English

JANUARY	FEBRUARY	MARCH	APRIL
MAY	JUNE	JULY	AUGUST
SEPTEMBER	OCTOBER	NOVEMBER	DECEMBER

My English Month: _________________________________

This month, I learned:

____

____

Put an x next to your answer

This month, I practiced English by:

Speaking _____

Writing _____

Listening _____

Reading _____

I practiced by:

____

____

New words I learned:

1. _________________________________

2. _________________________________

3. _________________________________

I feel proud because:

____

____

My next goal:

29

My English Progress Journey

Name: ______________________________ **Date:** _____________________

MONTH: What I practiced or learned in English

JANUARY	FEBRUARY	MARCH	APRIL
MAY	JUNE	JULY	AUGUST
SEPTEMBER	OCTOBER	NOVEMBER	DECEMBER

My English Month: _________________________________

This month, I learned:

____

____

Put an x next to your answer

This month, I practiced English by:

Speaking _____

Writing _____

Listening _____

Reading _____

I practiced by:

____

____

New words I learned:

1. _______________________________

2. _______________________________

3. _______________________________

I feel proud because:

____

____

My next goal:

____

Conclusion

It is important to keep going. Learning English is not easy. It takes time and patience. You may not always feel confident, and that's okay. You are allowed to make mistakes, because they help us to learn. Remember, this is YOUR journey and experience. Always try your best, because when you try your best, you DO YOUR BEST. Be proud of yourself for trying your best, one step at a time. 😊

GRAMMAR POINTS

Parts of Speech

Noun: people, places, things, animals, or an idea
Pronoun: replaces a noun
Example: I, me, you, we, us, they, them, he, his, she, her, it
Possessive pronouns (use to show ownership): my, his, her, our, their, theirs, your, yours
Example: My book. Her book. Your book. Their book. Our book.
Verb: an action word
Example: talk, listen, dance, watch, play
Adjective: a word that describes a noun
Example: beautiful, ugly, big, small, tall, short
Adverb: a word or phrase that describes, modifies, or quantifies an adjective, verb, or adverb. It can also express time, place, or a circumstance
*Most adverbs end in -ly
Example: really, randomly, abruptly, financially, quickly
For time (when and where something happened) or circumstances: here, often, there, everywhere, outside, inside, now, today, tomorrow, later
Preposition: connects a noun to another word
Example: at, after, to, on, but
Conjunction: joins sentences, words, or clauses together
Example: and, but, when
Example sentences: **When** I go to the doctor, I feel better.
We bought two shirts, three ties, **and** one coat.
He wants to go to school, **but** he doesn't feel well.

The is a definite article to talk about something specific. It is used before a noun
Interjection: short words or words with exclamation that are sometimes put in a sentence.
Example: Hi! Ouch! Oh! Well
Example sentence: Ouch! That hurts.

BE VERBS [am, is, are]
<u>BE verbs</u> are verbs that describe an action from people or things.

Subject + BE verb

I	**am**
You	**are**
We	**are**
They	**are**
He	**is**
She	**is**
It	**is**

Example: I am happy. He is hungry. We are tired.

Contractions

I am	**I'm**
You are	**You're**
We are	**We're**
They are	**They're**
He is	**He's**
She is	**She's**
It is	**It's**

(') is called an apostrophe
Use an apostrophe (') to make a contraction.

Negative:
Use *not* to make things negative
Example: I am *not* happy. We are *not* hungry. She is *not* tired.

Simple Present Tense and verbs in the third person (-s, -es, -ies)

We use the present tense when talking about things happening now.

Verb: talk

I	talk
You	talk
We	talk
They	talk
He	talks
She	talks
It	talks

With most verbs, we use **–s** when talking in the third person (he, she, it)
Example: Eat
He eat**s**, She eat**s**, It eat**s**

Verbs that have the following sounds: **s, z, ch, sh, x**, add **–es**
Example: Kis**s**= kisses
He kiss**es**, She kiss**es**, It kiss**es**

Buzz=buz**z**es
He buzz**es**, She buzz**es**, It buzz**es**

Tea**ch**=teaches
He teach**es**, She teach**es**, It teach**es**

Fini**sh**= finishes
He finish**es**, She finish**es**, It finish**es**

Fi**x**= fi**x**es
He fix**es**, She fix**es**, It fix**es**

Verbs that end in –y can also change to **–s** when it ends in one *vowel* + y
Example: play
"a" is a vowel
Play= plays
He plays, She plays, It plays

Verbs that end in –y can change into **–ies** if it ends with a *consonant* + y
Example: cry
"r" is a consonant
Cry= cries
He cr**ies**, she cr**ies**, it cr**ies**

Irregular verbs: verbs that do not follow the same rules as regular verbs.

Present	Past
go, goes	went
do, does	did
be	was, were
see	saw
eat	ate
become	became
feel	felt
fall	fell
break	broke
come	came
hurt	hurt
choose	chose
cut	cut
have, has	had
know	knew
lay	laid
give	gave
get	got
forgive	forgave
begin	began
drink	drank
bring	brought
make	made
read	read
let	let
lie	lay
hear	heard
meet	met
leave	left
run	ran
pay	paid
quit	quit
sell	sold
send	sent
sit	sat
ride	rode
fight	fought
teach	taught
steal	stole
understand	understood

think	thought
write	wrote
take	took
spend	spent
sleep	slept
speak	spoke

Vowels: a, e, i, o, u and sometimes y
Consonants: all letters except vowels. Y is also a consonant

BE VERBS in the Past Tense [was, were]

<u>BE verbs</u> in the past tense are verbs that describe an action from people or things in the past.

Subject + BE verb

I	**was**
You	**were**
We	**were**
They	**were**
He	**was**
She	**was**
It	**was**

Example: I was happy. He was hungry. We were tired.

<u>Negative</u>

Use ***not*** to make things negative. Use ***not*** after the verb.

Example: I was ***not*** happy.
We were ***not*** hungry.
She was ***not*** tired.

Simple Past Tense

We use the past tense when talking about things that happened in the past.

Verb: talk
Add **–ed** to the end of verbs for the past tense

I	**talk**ed
You	**talk**ed
We	**talk**ed
They	**talk**ed
He	**talk**ed
She	**talk**ed
It	**talk**ed

Verbs ending in **-e** (the –e is silent), add **–d**
Example: phone= phone**d**
*I phoned my friend. (British English)
I called my friend. (American English)

Close= close**d**
They closed the book.

Verbs ending in a *vowel*+ y, add **-ed**
Example: play= play**ed**
We played the game.

Verbs ending in a consonant+ y, add **-ied**
Example: marry= marr**ied**
She married her boyfriend.

Present Continuous

Present continuous is when something is happening now.

Subject + BE verb (am, is, are) + verb + -ing

Example: listen
I + am + listening.

Example: try
She + is + trying.

*Verb does not change in the third person.

Example: read
You + are + reading.

*Example: go
We use **going** with a <u>noun</u> (place) or verb (action)

I + am + going + to + <u>the supermarket</u>. (noun)

*to is a preposition that connects with the <u>noun</u>

They + are + going + <u>to listen</u>. (verb)

*Example: do
We + are + doing + <u>work</u>
We use **doing** with a <u>noun</u>

<u>Negative</u>
Use **not** to make things negative. Use **not** after the verb.

Example: I am **not** listening.
She is **not** trying.
You are **not** reading.
I am **not** going to the supermarket.
We are **not** doing work.

<u>Past Continuous</u>
Past continuous is when something is happening in the past.

Subject + BE verb (was, were) + verb + -ing

Example: speak
They + were + speaking.

Example: teach
I + was + teaching.

*Example: go
He + was+ going + <u>to the bedroom.</u> (place)
I + was + going <u>+ to think</u> (action)
When we use **going**, we include a verb (an action) or a noun (place)

*Example: do
They + were + doing + <u>homework.</u> (noun)
She + was + doing + <u>laundry.</u>
When we use **doing**, we include a <u>noun</u>

<u>Negative</u>
Use **not** to make things negative. Use **not** after the verb.

Example: There were not speaking.
I was not teaching.
He was not going to the bedroom.
I was not going to think.

Future tense

We use the future tense when talking about something in the future (something that did not happen yet).
We use **will** and **be going to** for the future tense.

We do not change the verb when using **will** or **be going to**

subject + will + verb (no change)

Example: study
I + will + study.

Example: travel
They + will + travel

Example: watch
He + will + watch *TV*.

*Sometimes we can add a *noun* at the end of the sentence

Negative

Use **not** to make things negative. Use **not** after will.

Example: I will **not** study.
They will **not** travel.
He will **not** watch TV.

subject + be going to + verb (no change)

Example: see
We + are going to + see + <u>a movie</u>. (noun)

Example: listen
I + am going to + listen + <u>to music</u>.

Example: read
He + is going to + read+ <u>a book</u>.

When using **be going to**, we can add a noun at the end of a sentence

<u>**Negative**</u>
Use *not* to make things negative. Use **not** after the BE verb.

Example: We are **not** going to see a movie.
I am **not** going to listen to music.
He is **not** going to read a book.

Present Perfect Tense

We use the present perfect tense to talk about an event that happened in the past but the result is in the present.

Subject + have/has + past participle

Example: I *have* <u>been</u> to New York.
This means you went to New York sometime in the past.

Example: She *has* <u>talked</u> to her friend.
This means she talked to her friend sometime in the past.

Negative

Use *not* to make things negative. Use **not** after have or has

Example: I have **not** been to New York.
She has **not** talked to her friend.

Subject	Have/ has	Past participle
I	have	These verbs have the –ed ending or are irregular
We	have	
You	have	
They	have	
He	**has**	
She	**has**	
It	**has**	

***Some verbs in past participle will be same in present and/or past tense**

These are just a few examples of verbs in the past participle

Verb	Past Participle
talk	talked
listen	listened
walk	walked
study	studied
play	played
read	read
hurt	hurt
let	let
run	run
quit	quit
go	gone
be	been
do	done

see	seen
eat	eaten
become	become
begin	begun
give	given
choose	chosen
feel	felt
lay	laid
say	said
speak	spoken
pay	paid
take	taken
sell	sold
understand	understood
write	written
think	thought
teach	taught
sit	sat

We can include **time** *(since, for)* when talking in the present perfect

Subject + have/has + past participle + time

Since is used to state a specific time

I **have** <u>watched</u> the show **since** 10 o'clock.
He **has** <u>taught</u> class *since* yesterday.

For is used to state time (not specific)

We **have** <u>lived</u> in the United States *for* 12 years.
It **has** <u>been</u> raining *for* 3 days.

Negative
I have **not** watched the show *since* 10 o'clock.
He has **not** taught class *since* yesterday.
We have **not** lived in the United States *for* 12 years.
It has **not** been raining *for* 3 days.

'Wh' Questions

What- to ask about information
Example: What is your name?

When- to ask about time (time, day, week, month, year)
Example: When is the doctor's appointment?

Who- to ask about a person or people
Example: Who is the teacher?

Where- to ask about place
Example: Where is the restaurant?

Why- to ask about a reason
Example: Why are you applying for a job?

Which- to compare, to choose
Example: Which shirt do you want to buy?

Yes/ No Questions

Be verb (Am, Is, Are…?)

Example: **Am** I a teacher?
Answer: Yes you **are**. No, you **are not** (No you **aren't**)

Are you a student?
Yes I **am**. No, I **am not** (No, **I'm not**)

Is he a student?
Yes he **is**. No, he **is not**. (No, **he's not** *or* No, he **isn't**)

Is she a student?
Yes she **is**. No, she **is not**. (No, **she's not** *or* No, she **isn't**)

Do or Does…?

I	**do**
You	**do**
We	**do**
They	**do**
He	**does**
She	**does**
It	**does**

Example: **Do** you go to school?

Answer: Yes I **do**. No, I **do not** or No, I **don't**.

Does she go to school?
Yes she **does**. No, she **does not** or No, she **doesn't**.

Will…?

I	will
You	will
We	will
They	will
He	will
She	will
It	will

Example: **Will** you find a job?
Answer: Yes I **will**. No, I **will not** or No, I **won't**.

Will he find a job?
Yes he **will**. No, he **will not** or No, he **won't**.

Will they find a job?
Yes they **will**. No, they **will not** or No, they **won't**.

Will not= won't (contraction)

Modals

Modals are words that express permission, ability, obligation, possibility, advice, probability, prohibition (warning/cannot do something), lack of necessity (not a must)

Modal	Meaning
Can	Ability, permission, possibility
Could	Possibility, permission (polite), ability in the past
May	Permission, possibility, probability
Might	Permission (polite), possibility, probability
Will	Possibility (future)
Would	Permission (polite), possibility
Should, ought to	Advice, some obligation, conclusion
Shall	Make offers, suggestions, advice
Had better	advice
Must	Strong obligation, certainty
Must not	Prohibition
Need not	Lack of necessity/no obligation

We use **can**, **could**, **may**, **will**, **would**, and **shall** when asking questions.

Example: Can you help me?
Could you help me? (polite, more formal)
May I take your order? (polite, formal)
Will you go to the interview?
Would you like to buy the dress?
Shall we take the bus?

Teacher Dara says:

TRY YOUR BEST